Shamrocks and Shepherds

FEDERAL Judge John Kilkenny was the ideal person to undertake this historical account. It was his own father's wish that the story of the Irish at work and at play in Morrow County, Oregon be gathered and written down. John Kilkenny was the man to do it, for this robust story is a part of the son's life too.

With the best of all timing he was in the right place to amass the ephemeral pieces and at the right moment to give it the keen eye and humor the zesty story deserves.

Sheep, cattle, and horses were right for the rolling hills of Morrow County—and so were the Irish land lookers. As he observes so truly the young Irish looking for work and opportunity in the American dream came as greenhorns, but they stayed to "put their extraordinary talents of mind and heart to work in the common goal of planting a civilization."

Thomas Vaughan

Shamrocks and Shepherds:
The Irish of Morrow County

by

John F. Kilkenny

To my Irish friends:

Well knowing your penchant for sharp-tongued invective, I am also aware of your tolerance. Please withhold the sting of your tongue, while exploring the breadth of your clemency.

Special Acknowledgements

I am particularly indebted to the following for the assistance and encouragement they have given over the years:

James Daly, Pendleton, Oregon
Elsie Fitzmaurice Dickson, Pendleton, Oregon
Mr. & Mrs. B. P. Doherty, Pendleton, Oregon
Andrew Donohue, deceased
John F. Kenny, deceased
W. P. Kilkenny, Pendleton, Oregon
Edward MacLysaght, Dublin, Ireland
Hugh O'Rourke, Heppner, Oregon
Bernard Ward, deceased

Second edition, revised
Copyright © 1981
Oregon Historical Society
Portland, Oregon

Library of Congress Catalog Card Number 81-83140
ISBN 0-87595-099-X

This work is inscribed to the haloed memory of my father and mother, John Sheridan and Rose Ann Kilkenny.

John S. Kilkenny, 1914 (Author's collection).

JOHN F. KILKENNY

Shamrocks and Shepherds: The Irish of Morrow County

Blue are the mountains of Morrow,
Green are its valleys and hills.
Lofty its peaks, and grassy its plains,
Its winters mean blizzards and chills.
Then come the springs and the summers,
With sunshine and flowers galore.
The livestock are fat and the wheat fields are gold,
Thank God for abundance, and more.

FROM the pages of history, we find that the wandering Celt has been on the constant move, ever westward, with few exceptions, from his known beginning in the twilight of the early European drama of man. As a result of a tragic history, to the ends of the earth have gone the O'Neils, the O'Dohertys, the O' Rourkes, the O'Kenneys, the O'Sullivans, the O'Donovans, the O'Briens, the O'Kennedys, the O'Carrolls, the O'Fogartys, the O'Kavanaughs, the O'Sheas, the O'Mahoneys, the O'Reillys, the O'Foleys, the McCartys, the McDermotts, the McMahons, the Maguires, the Kildares, the Kilkennys, the Kilbrides, the Kilpatricks, the Fitzmaurices, the Fitzgibbons, the Fitzpatricks, the Fitzsimmons, and hundreds of other families of pure Irish stock. Nostalgically proud of their family names and of their ancestors, the wandering Celts have supplied to each of their adopted countries an exciting ancestral background, unequaled by any other national group. Is there a nation on the face of the earth whose history has not recorded the valor, the courage, the music, the social grace, the humor, the intellectual brilliance, and the drinking ability and inability, of this race of happy warriors whose wars were merry and whose songs were sad?

[5]

This work would not be meaningful without some reference to the Celtic part in the American Revolution, the War of 1812, the great migration through Cumberland Gap, the Lewis and Clark expedition, the Hudson's Bay Company, the mountain men, the miners, the canal builders, the massive western push of the American railroad, to all of which the Irish made a colossal contribution.

As to the part played by the Irish immigrant in early American history, I need only quote from an address by Irvin S. Cobb to the American-Irish Historical Society on January 6, 1917, as follows: "As for Daniel Boone, the Great Pathfinder, he really was descended from the line of Buhun, which is Norman-Irish, and his mother was a Morgan, his wife a Bryan and his father was an Irish Catholic." And from a statement of President Theodore Roosevelt to the same group on January 16, 1909: "You perform a noble work in bringing to light the history of the Irish people in this country, particularly the achievements of those early immigrants who came from Ireland long before the outbreak of the Revolution and planted themselves as the advance guard of a conquering civilization on the border of the Indian-haunted wilderness . . . And I am proud of the strain of Irish blood in my veins."

From Ireland came Celtic thousands pouring into the Middle West, the Great Plains, the Lone Star state, the Spanish possessions, the Oregon Country and the Rocky Mountains. In each area and in each state they immortalized their names on the mountain peaks and the valleys below, the roaring streams and the placid lakes, the wagon roads and the railway towns, the corner saloons and the general store, the battlefields and the shrines of death.

> A mortal little island,
> No other land or clime,
> Has placed more deathless heroes,
> In the pantheon of time.*

With their bare hands and splendid physiques, their sweaty brows and steadfast eyes, their ready wit and musical hearts, our august Celtic progenitors gouged the then wondrous Erie and

---

*Author unknown.

[6]

Rose Ann Kilkenny

other canals out of the wilderness; and shortly thereafter, molded the earth, timber and the steel that formed the basis of the construction of the great transcontinental railway systems, which served to populate the West.

Rumor has it that the reason the experts have had so much difficulty in tracing the origin of the name "Oregon" is that the area was discovered, long before the advent of the Indian, by a wandering group of Celts under the command of one Michael Patrick O'Regon. Doubters have failed to disprove this most plausible suggestion, and theirs, I feel, is the burden of proof.

On their westward journey they left their imprints on hundreds of communities such as Limerick, Maine; Dublin, New Hampshire; Galway, New York; Kilarney, West Virginia; Kilkenny, Minnesota; St. Patrick, Missouri; Shamrock, Texas; Cody, Wyoming; O'Brien, California; Irish Bend, Murphy,

Bandon, Aloysius, Kelleher and St. Patrick's Peak, Oregon.

Riding to their death on the Little Big Horn, with the gallant but reckless Custer, were those with the Gaelic names of: Moody, McDonald, Sullivan, Doran, Harrington, Foley, Ryan, Shea, Hagan, Harnington, Kavaugh, Mahoney, O'Connell, Butler, Walsh, Burke, McGue, McCarthy, Dugan, Galvin, Callahan, Keogh, Patton, Bailey, Barry, Conners, Downing, McElroy, Mooney, Boyle, Farrell, O'Conner, Kenney, Briody, Brandon, Atchison, Brady, Carney, Donnelly, Driscoll, Kelley, McIchargey, Mitchell, O'Bryan, Quinn, Considine, Martin, McGinniss and O'Hara.

Of the foreigners who have won the Congressional Medal of Honor, approximately 50% or 111 are Irishmen. Their numbers exceed the combined total of England, Scotland, Wales, Germany, Canada, Russia and France.

The principal characters around whom spun the dramatic influx of the Irish into Morrow County were comparatively few in number. The first to plant a firm foot in the Heppner area was William Hughes, who arrived around 1870. Not far behind was the dedicated Charlie Cunningham, who filed his pre-emption claim on Butter Creek in 1876. In the eighties came Felix Johnson, Jeremiah Brosnan, Michael Kenny, Patrick, B. P. and James G. Doherty, to settle and then welcome John Kilkenny and James Carty[1] in 1890. These, with the help of a few others, were the men who bore the heavy burden of providing the cost of transportation for the waiting friends and relatives in Ireland. They were the stalwarts upon whose shoulders was placed the task of providing a livelihood for the greenhorns. This livelihood they did provide, and in turn, the greenhorns became ranchers and put the power of their earnings to the never ending stream of incoming Gaelic blood. To all of the early explorers, their descendants are eternally grateful and carry their names with a pride known only to the Irish.

Of the 1890 arrivals mentioned, John Sheridan Kilkenny was born in County Leitrim, Ireland, on May 14, 1870, the son of Peter and Mary Ann (Sheridan) Kilkenny. Mary Ann was in America in the late 1870s and early 1880s. Peter was in America

---

1. Portland General Electric powerplant at Boardman was named for James Carty.

in the early 1880s. Both trips were made to obtain funds to support the family. They lived in both New York and Boston on those occasions. Other children were Ellen, Rose, Bridget, Sarah, Katherine, Frank, Patrick and Peter. All came to America with the exception of Sarah.

Jim Carty and John Kilkenny arrived at Umatilla, Oregon, via the Oregon R. & N. line, in May 1890. They had learned of a few Irishmen at Heppner and made their way there by foot from Umatilla. The first night they spent in the vicinity of the present Kilkenny ranch on Butter Creek, the second at the forks of Sand Hollow and the third reached Heppner. At first they were employed on the completion of the branch line of the railroad at Heppner. On their arrival they became acquainted with William (Bill) Hughes, a native of County Tipperary. Bill had been in California for a number of years and had been very successful as a merchant and stock grower in the Heppner area. He had money to loan and started John and Jim in the sheep business in 1892 or 1893. It was not long before they acquired three or four bands of sheep and took up a permanent residence in Sand Hollow at the site later known as the old Kilkenny ranch.[2] In a few years they included in the partnership John Sheridan, another immigrant from County Leitrim. They operated as partners for a number of years and on the dissolution Jim moved his headquarters to what was known as Tub Springs in Juniper Canyon. Sheridan sold his interest and returned to Ireland and married Bridget Brady. About this time, Jim and John married sisters, Maria and Rose Ann Curran. Jim returned to Ireland to marry Maria and John married Rose Ann, one of God's noblewomen, in Heppner in 1898. Rose Ann had been previously married to Luke Farley, who was killed in an accident, leaving Rose Ann with a son, Patrick Gregory, who died in 1932. Both John and Jim were successful in the sheep business. In the early days, the bunch grass was so abundant in the north end of Morrow County that it was unnecessary to arrange for winter feed. John's brothers, Frank and Pat, were with him at the turn of the century and for some years thereafter, when they went to Ireland, Frank returning to Morrow County in the late twenties.

---

2. Original Patent, December 1, 1898, Book E. of Patents, p. 5, Morrow County Records.

Maria Curran Carty and James Carty in 1898 (Author's collection).

Those were the delightful days of greyhounds and man against the wily coyote. John acquired a pack of greyhounds, his favorites being the massive Johnson, the fleet Grey Boy and the smaller Brindle. On Sunday morning, it was "off to the hunt," he astride Black Paddy, a magnificent black horse of Arabian and Morgan blood. Joining in the hunt, on most occasions, was Rev. T. J. Hoskins, who lived at Pine City and hunted with a team and hack. He transported his hounds in cages until the coyote was sighted.

With the increase in number of sheep, cattle and horses, to say nothing of millions of jack rabbits, the winter feed supply started to collapse, and it was necessary, about the year 1908 or 1909, to commence buying hay, the closest supply being on Butter Creek. The sheep were moved to the mountain range during the summer. In the earlier days, it was first come, first served, with a defense of your rights by fist or gun. The Irish, knowing little or nothing about the use of a gun, were under somewhat of a handicap, except for the close-in fighting. At that form of this masculine pleasure, they were superb. For many years his summer range was in and around Indian Creek and there is still one area on that creek which is known as Kilkenny Crossing. During this time the sheep-cattle wars were going on throughout the West and on one occasion John, Jim and Frank Kilkenny engaged in a Donnybrook with the cattlemen on Indian Creek. Hundreds of the sheep were shot during the course of this fight.

About 1910, John started expanding his operations, buying what was commonly known as the W. B. Finley rangeland. In 1911, Rose Ann started asserting her rights and built a prodigious new home in Sand Hollow. In the meantime, she had taken her family, then consisting of Rose Ellen, Johnny, Sarah and Bill, to Ireland for a visit. On their return, John made a trip to Ireland and returned before the birth of Mary Ann.

A long-time director and officer of the First National Bank of Heppner, he was also very active politically and was a director and chairman of the board of the Alpine Public School District. The schoolhouse was located approximately one mile south of the ranch house and this distance was walked by the

Kilkenny Hinton Creek Ranch in 1914, with ranch house, blacksmith shop, smoke house and barn (Author's collection).

children each day. Likewise, he was interested in county politics, serving as a county commissioner for a number of years. His contribution of $5,000 to the campaign of Senator Robert N. Stanfield received wide publicity.

In 1914, John had visions of a ranching empire and in the the spring of that year acquired the George Currin ranch southeast of Heppner, this ranch consisting of more than 20,000 acres of fine bunch grass, dry farm and alfalfa land. On February 15, 1915, tragedy struck the family as Rose Ann was killed in an elevator accident in Pendleton. Aunt Mary, a lady of quality, joined her brother and assisted in taking care of the family for a number of years. Lottie Russell, daughter of Gilliam County pioneers, and John were married in February, 1917. Another truly great woman. To them were born Ilene, Colleen and Robert Emmett, all now residing in Morrow County.

In 1918, his land ownings were again enlarged by the purchase of a huge tract of summer grazing land on the middle fork of the John Day River in the Galena-Whiskey Flat area, and in 1920 the final rounding out of an ideal stock ranch by the purchase of what was known as the Bowman alfalfa ranch on Butter Creek. The operation of these ranches continued until the start of the Depression in 1930, when the Oregon Lumber Company demanded final payment of the amount due on the mountain ranch, which he was unable to make. John lost this ranch and its fine stand of timber.

During these fifteen empire years, he was running from 10,000 to 12,000 head of ewes, 1,500 to 2,500 head of yearling wethers and 250 to 350 head of cattle. After lambing, the total number of sheep increased to over 20,000 and the cattle, would, after calving, increase by 150 to 200 head. Subsequent to 1918, the summer range in Oregon was insufficient. He then grazed thousands of head of sheep at out-of-state points, including Elk City and Grangeville, Idaho, Thompson Falls and the Crow Reservation in Montana. Generally speaking, these sheep were grazed in transit, on their way to market in Chicago. The ewes, however, were returned to the home ranges in the fall. As the absolute ruler of this vast domain, it would be difficult to guess the humble origin of his County Leitrim birth. Indeed,

> The hills were white with the sheep of our Father,
> The valleys were brown with his cattle.
> The horses did neigh at the dogs who would stray,
> As they shied at the snakes with a rattle.

John was a leader in most all of his enterprises. He was the first to drill a deep water well in the north end of Morrow County; the first to use a gasoline engine in lieu of a windmill; the first of the Irish to own and drive an automobile. (His early training required that he say "Whoa" to the vehicle throughout his life.) He was one of the first to use power-driven sheep-shearing machinery. One of the first to use small tractors in farm operations. The first to install electricity in the ranch house and barn. One of the first to install a telephone. One of the first to make "home brew" during Prohibition days, and one of the first to drink it. One of the first to install central furnace heating in the ranch house.

On occasion, a man of terrible temper, a fighter at the drop of a hat—he could curse his luck with a fluency that made

[13]

normal profanity seem quite commonplace—for the most part he was a very kind and considerate person. It has been said that the Depression would never have affected his operations, had it not been for the many outstanding negotiable instruments which he had signed as a guarantor for others. The thousands and thousands of dollars he was compelled to pay on these gestures of friendship, were the dollars that were the difference between survival and partial ruin. His insistence that his children attend college ran contrary to the main stream of the rancher thinking of the time. Rose, Johnny, Sarah, Bill, Mary Ann and Ilene attended college. Bob and Colleen did not have this advantage. Only lack of available funds prevented their attendance.

He delighted in arguing the controversial issues of the day. Somewhat of a heckler, he would deliberately lure the unsuspecting onto an impossible prong of a dilemma. Newspapers were his Bible. Each edition was read from front to rear, making him one of the best-read men of his area. Speaking of the Bible, John, although a very substantial contributor to the church, was on most occasions casting a rather critical eye on the parish priest. This attitude mellowed with the advance of age, so that for many years before his death he was a very devoted person.

His battles with the demon rum were many, bardic, forensic and exhausting. Through his early fifties he could and did hold his liquor with the best. Thereafter, his drinking became a problem and he solved it by going on approximately two "tears" a year. For months he would have none of it, then would partake of a few social drinks, the few became many and finally, all within a period of weeks, he would complete the cycle and go back on the wagon. His most apt expression, when refusing a drink: "It's a bad dog you have to muzzle." During Prohibition days, while on one of the many fun parties with a group of friends, one of them asked what he thought of Prohibition. With the usual twinkle in his eyes, he replied: "It's better than no whisky at all."

In his social, economic and political contacts with others, high or low, he was the image by which the community knew the Irish: completely approachable, courteous until provoked, first to reach a helping hand, utter a kindly word, partake of a friendly drink, or engage in a worthwhile fight.

His industry was prodigious. Throughout his life he arose between 5:00 and 5:30 a.m. He drove his workmen and children, but he did not spare himself. His impatience with the indolent was matched only by his patience with the willing performer. John Kilkenny was no ordinary man. He certainly belongs in the front ranks of great livestock men of his or any other time.

To him, we children are deeply indebted for the wisdom and humility of his parenthood, and the courageousness and decisiveness of his actions.

The panic of the early 1930s placed him in such a financial condition that he had to sacrifice massive segments of his real and personal property in order to preserve those parts which he transferred to members of his family. Those remnants of his vast empire, to put it modestly, have substantial value on the present market. That which was lost would, without livestock, be valued well in the millions. The timber alone, on the Susanville ranch, would have a fantastic value.

In 1938, he noticed a growth on the left side of his cheek. This developed into a malignancy and he was placed in St. Anthony's Hopital in Pendleton in the fall of 1939. On the occasion of his last automobile ride, we took him from the hospital to the Butter Creek ranch. At his request, we drove to his old homestead in Sand Hollow and thence to the top of Finley Buttes, with a magnificent view of the towering Cascades, where he left the car and faced to the north, the east, thence south and west. There he stood, a stout exemplar of the Latin phrase, *ad summa vertus* (courage to the last), looking out over a substantial segment of his once vast domain—then old and stooped and dying, yet pathetically magnificent, a glowing tribute to himself and to the grandeur of a monumental past.

With the left side of his jaw completely gone, he went to his God in the presence of most of his family on November 29, 1939, almost fifty years from first setting foot on the beloved soil of Morrow County. After one of the largest funerals in that county's history, he was placed at rest beside Rose Ann in the cemetery on the hill overlooking the city, where he started his meteoric rise some half a century before.

[15]

How Irish was he? He was deeply and wholesomely and wholly Irish. There is no use in saying he was as Irish as the Book of Kells, nor as Irish as an evening spent in a Dublin public house, nor even as the man who destroyed Nelson's statue in Dublin Square. These references do not truly show how Irish he was. But this might: if a century from now someone else would say, that he, or she, is as Irish as John Kilkenny.

Many years before my father died he emphasized the necessity of someone undertaking the task of perpetuating the names of the Irish families responsible, in good measure, for the early settlement of Morrow County. From time to time, in the past fifteen years, I have been gathering information, but still feel that the names presented in this work do not exhaust the subject and that the list is quite inadequate and incomplete. Many of the young Irishmen who spent their lonely nights and busy days on the ranches and in the mountains, made sufficient money to purchase a small plot in Ireland and returned to their native land to find the girls of their choice. The Irish influx to this part of the West was approximately 85 per cent boys and 15 per cent girls. As a result, most of the men lived very monastic lives and a tragically large percentage of those who remained in America, lived and died bachelors.

Along the Oregon Trail, as it traversed Morrow County, both before and after the turn of the century, the countryside was dotted with the livestock ranches of the Irish, including, among others, the Cartys, James and Con; the Connells, Jim and Pat; the Currans, John, Pat and Pete; the Devlins, Barney and Mike; the Dohertys, Little Barney, Neil, Jim, Big Pat and Red Pat; the Donohues, Andy and Mike; the Farleys, Jim and Pete; the Flanagans, Pat and Frank; the Healys, John, Mike and Pat; the Hughes, William, John and Matt; the Kennys, Mike, John and Barney, the Kilkennys, John, Pat and Frank; the McCabes, Frank, Mike and Luke; the McDaids, Ed and Jerry; the Mc-Devitts, Barney, John and Dan; the McEntires, Johnny, Jim and Pete; the McNamees, James, John and Dennis; the Marshalls,

John and Michael; the Monahans, Frank and John; the Murphys, Bill and Dan; the O'Connors, Jeremiah, James and Tim; the O'Rourkes, Hughie and John; the Quaids, Tom, Mike and Pat, and the Sheridans, John and James.

The controlling Irish influence in the area, at the time, is emphasized by the now forgotten fact that the Heppner High School athletic teams, for over a quarter of a century, were known as the "Irish." Also forgotten in the area is the once powerful influence of the Ancient Order of Hibernians, Heppner being home of the second largest lodge in the State of Oregon. Numerically, the Irish were by far the most numerous ethnic group in the district.

Under their ownership, management and control were literally hundreds of thousands of sheep, thousands of cattle and horses, and later, thousands upon thousands of acres of farm land. The Oregon Trail, dramatically carved by countless thousands of hoofs and wheels, actually severed the ranch lands of the Cartys, the Dohertys, the Farleys, the Flanagans, the Kilkennys, the McDaids, the McEntires and the Sheridans.

All men of energy, dedication and resolution, they handled their assignments with a consummate skill which led to results that were both dramatic and convincing. The profound influence of music, song,[3] laughter and, at times, downright hilarity, left a lifelong mark which reflected itself in the grand emphasis placed by their offspring on these priceless arts of living.

My childhood memories bring back one typically glamorous New Year's Eve and Day. Throughout the year the herders, camp tenders and ranch hands led spartan and lonely lives. An exception was New Year's Eve and New Year's Day when all, or practically all, of the livestock were on feed or close to the main ranch. One occasion I recall occured in 1911 and was in celebration of the opening of the new home which Father

---

3. Some of the Irish songs sung on the Kilkenny ranches in Morrow County were: The Harp that once through Tara's Halls, My Wild Irish Rose, Mother Machree, Kathleen Mavourneen, The Wearing of the Green, The Bells of Shandon, The Irish Washerwoman, Come Back to Erin, Dear Old Donegal, Where the River Shannon Flows, The Minstrel Boy, Let Erin Remember the Days of Old, Believe Me if All Those Endearing Young Charms, Tumble Down Shack in Athlone, Remember the Glories of Brien the Brave, 'Tis the last Rose of Summer, When Irish Eyes are Smiling (a comparative latecomer), Kelly with the Green Necktie, By Killarney's Lakes and Dells.

and Mother had built in Sand Hollow. For the times and the area it was nothing less than a mansion, containing approximately 5,000 square feet of floor space, not to speak of the attic or the basement. As with the courthouse of the day, the full front verandah faced to the west. On this occasion, the beer and whisky flowed quite freely. As a result, numerous of the employees suffered casualties of such a nature that they were entirely incapacitated the following day, much to the displeasure of my father and the hunger of the livestock. Jim McEntire took his place at the breakfast table with two broken shoulders and was unable to bring a cup of coffee to his lips. John Sheridan used his teeth on the forefinger of Private Dundass to such an extent as to require major surgery, but the Private did not lose the finger until he partially removed, in a rather unsurgical manner, a substantial portion of Sheridan's tonsils, thus rendering the latter sore and speechless for several weeks. Other hands sustained injuries sufficiently severe and noticeable, to *prima facie* establish the fact that their backs were not turned on the joyful combats of the previous evening. I dimly remember Dad shouting to one of the particularly annoying belligerents, "By Jesus, fellow, I threw you out of the house an hour ago, and now, damn your soul, I shall do it again!" And he did.

Morrow County is a better place in which to live by reason of the efforts of the hundreds of Irish boys and a few Irish girls who put their extraordinary talents of mind and heart to work in the common goal of planting a civilization in the then thin edge of a wilderness. Only those familiar with the guttural, but hair-raising grunt of the black bear, the fascinating, but blood-curdling howl of the timber wolf and the lonesome, but terrifying scream of the cougar, can fully appreciate the paralyzing fear which crept into the hearts of these courageous greenhorns as they spent their first forlorn nights in the empty stillness of the precipitous canyons and lofty spaces of the mountains they conquered and grew to love and which are now commonly known as the Blue.

In the Celtic community of my youth, it was a mark of cowardice to carry a sixshooter. All controversy was settled by fists. The grudge, so frequently pictured in today's "Old West," was entirely unknown. The bloody adversaries of tonight were

[18]

About 1,000 rabbits destroyed in this Morrow County rabbit drive (OHS collections).

the laughing companions of tomorrow. Woe to him who might suggest a reference to the night before.

To them, of course, a good rough and tumble fight was a delightful form of exercise and test of physical prowess, rather than a violation of law. With such a philosophy, it is quite understandable that a goodly number could never appreciate why these moments of pleasure were rudely interrupted by a town marshal or county sheriff under pretense of law enforcement.

Of our Celtic ancestors we are rightfully proud. Proud of the Irish names they gave us; proud of the life and joy they provided in our youth, proud of the education on which they insisted, and above all we are proud of the hard core of Celtic toughness, deeply rooted, thus enabling us to meet, endure, withstand and live with the everyday problems of human existence.

Blessed as they were with a humorous sense of self-esteem and a practical foresight second to none, they adapted well to to a spartan existence on the ever solitary plains and in the austere and forbidding mountains of their chosen land. Each was a thesaurus of wit, song, companionship, belligerency, affection, sentiment and emotion.

> The fun and the frolic, prevented the colic,
> In the immigrant Irish of yore.
> Inborn was their mirth, 'twas with them since birth,
> And was bred in the bone to the core.

The stories of their impatience with the dull-witted are legend. Their unbridled impetuosity and overpowering urge to finish quickly the principal features of their work, and leave the details to others, detract in some measure, from their overall ability to cope with the precise problem at hand. But finish the job they did. Besides being men of honesty, courage and integrity, they were also men of charm and humility, qualities which were extremely helpful in an utterly strange and some-times hostile community.

Though mostly Catholic in religion, a substantial number were Protestants. Religious intolerance was nonexistent. At least three Irish Protestants, Henry Dennis, Pat Hart and Harry Mulligan, worked on the Kilkenny ranches at the same time. The first Catholic church was constructed in the area at Vinson, approximately 30 miles east of Heppner. This was a small, rough slab wood building, built entirely by the Irish families in the neighborhood. Both Catholics and non-Catholics alike contributed the labor, materials and money for the construction, in 1887, of the first Catholic church in Heppner. The building committee included William Hughes, James Hager and William MacAtee, all non-Catholics. Naturally, the church was dedicated to and named for St. Patrick. Substantial contributors included Henry Heppner, the Jewish merchant after whom the city was named, and Phill Cohn, a pioneer Jewish warehouseman and trader.[4] The first recorded marriage in the church was that of John Kilkenny and Rose Ann Curran Farley.

---

4. Not until the Ku Klux Klan raised its ugly head in the mid-twenties did the community become conscious of a variance in religious beliefs.

[20]

Irish Nomenclature

Irish surnames may be classified as: (1) Gaelic, (2) Gaelic-Norman, and (3) Anglo-Norman. The O and the Mac originally played a significant role in the formation of each of the classes. Most of the common names carried either the O or the Mac. Simply stated O signified "of" the ancestral group, while Mac implied "son of."

In general, Gaelic is a reference to the language of the Irish, although variants of the Gaelic are also spoken by the Highland Scots, the Welsh, a small group of the Cornish and some of the inhabitants of Brittany. Fundamentally, Celtic refers to the blood strain of the person, as distinguished from Norman, Anglo-Norman, or English. Although the proper pronunciation is "keltic," the name, in America, is commonly pronounced with a soft s.

Before the introduction of surnames in Ireland, a system of clan names, which the use of surnames gradually rendered obsolete, was existent. Many groups of families descended from a common ancestor and these were known by collective clan names, such as Dal Cais, Ui Maine (or Hy Many), Cinel Eoghain, Clann Cholgain, and others. Tribe names, as used by O'Donovan, are possibly more expressive, although this is disputed by some authorities.

In the seventeenth century, the dire affects of the partial Anglo-Norman Conquest were greatly intensified by the Plantation of Ulster, the Cromwellian Settlement and the Williamite Forfeitures, followed, of course, by the Penal Code. One of the principal effects of the Penal Code was the wholesale discarding of the distinctive prefixes O and Mac. Even the great Daniel O'Connell, as late as 1803, was signing his name as Connell, while the chief of the MacDermotts signed himself simply as Anthony Dermott. Many people outside of Ireland are of the belief that Mac is essentially a Scottish prefix. There is no validity to this claim, as many of the foremost Irish families such as MacCarthy, MacDermott, MacGrath, MacGillicuddy, MacKenna, MacMahon, MacNamara and literally dozens of others use this prefix. Neither the Irish, nor the Scots, distinguish between Mc and Mac.

At the beginning of the present century, a general reversal of the process began to show itself and many of the old Irish names have again taken the O and the Mac. The thought that the prefix Fitz always denotes a Norman origin, is generally true. An exception is Fitzpatrick, which was to the seventeenth century, MacGilpatrick. Fitz comes from the French word *fils*. But even the names Fitzgerald, Fitzgibbon and Fitzmaurice must be regarded as Irish. Not only have they been continuously in Ireland for eight or more centuries, but they cannot be found in England, except where introduced by Irish settlers.

Family Names: The Irish of Morrow County[4]

Blessing: Joe Blessing arrived in Morrow County after 1910 and worked for John Kilkenny and a number of others prior to his unfortunate death by gunshot in the late twenties. He was born in Cloone, County Leitrim, Ireland.

O'Bohan: Pat Bohan was born in County Leitrim and arrived shortly after 1910, worked for John Kilkenny for a great many years and later for M. S. Corrigal, an outstanding Scottish livestock man and Irish benefactor.

O'Bonar: John Bonar was born in County Donegal and worked on livestock ranches in Morrow County for a number of years.

O'Brady, O'Grady: Father T. J. Brady served in Heppner with Father George Hennessy in the Chapel Car St. Anthony shortly after the turn of the century. He returned to the parish in Heppner in January 1928, and served for a short period of time.

John, Patrick and Phil Brady, brothers, were born in County Cavan, worked for a great many years and some of the brothers were employed by C. A. Minor, Phil marrying Blanche, one of Minor's daughters.

Johnny Brady was born in County Leitrim, as was Lawrence Brady. Each of them worked for John Kilkenny, Mike Kenny and others. Ellen Brady, wife of John Sheridan, was born in County Leitrim.

Brannock: Virginia Brannock Kilkenny, wife of Judge John F. Kilkenny, and her brother, Robert, were rather latecomers in joining the group. Ginny's first visit to the area was in the mid or late twenties, at which time she caught the eye of John F. Born to this union were Michael and Karen. Mike married Julie King, daughter of a prominent Umatilla County family, and to this union were born Nancy, Michael Lester, Christopher, Pattie and Ellen. To Karen's union with T. K. Klosterman, Jr., were born Katie K. and Ginny B. and Frederick.

O'Brennan, Mac Brennan: Tommy Brennan was a blacksmith, having learned his trade in Dublin. He sailed the seas for many years before taking up his profession in Heppner around 1900. Unremitting in his pursuit of perfection, he had an uncanny knowledge of stresses and strains in wagonwheels. Craftsmanship, not technology, was the tool of his trade, and it was the tightness of the joints, not glue, that keep his wheels from coming apart.

Dr. J. P. Brennan, while having his office in Pendleton, had and still has as his patients a substantial number of the Irish of Morrow

---

5. Morrow County and its environs. With few exceptions those listed here arrived between 1870 and 1910, of whom more than 90 percent were not over 21 years of age.

County. His wife carries on the tradition by using as her given name that historical Irish surname Creagh.

O'Breslin: Ed Breslin, long-time merchant in Heppner, was born in County Leitrim.

O'Briody: Father Thomas Briody, chaplain at St. Joseph's Academy in Pendleton for a number of years after 1893, rode horseback to Heppner on Sundays to say Mass. He officiated at the marriage ceremony of John Sheridan Kilkenny and Rose Ann Curran Farley in Heppner in 1898.

Brosnan: Jeremiah Brosnan was born in County Cork, Ireland, and arrived, around the Horn, in the Morrow County area in the 1870s, and soon met Mary Gafney to whom he was married in 1881. She came to this country with Michael Kenny and was a sister of Kate Johnson, the wife of Felix Johnson, all herein mentioned. Jerry was one of the outstanding characters of his time, a wit, satirist and great cattleman. His progeny have honored his name by being quite successful on their own. Kate, one of his daughters, was a bridesmaid at the John Kilkenny-Rose Ann Curran wedding in Heppner in 1898.

Burke: Jack Burke worked for John Sheridan and John Kilkenny for a great many years. His ancestral area in Ireland is unknown.

O'Byrne: John Byrne arrived in Morrow County in the early part of the century from County Leitrim. His sister, Margaret Byrne, married Patrick Farley, later mentioned. John was an author and a poet of sorts with extremely positive political views.

Frank Byrne arrived in Morrow County about the same time from the same county in Ireland.

O'Cain, O'Kane: Jim Cain, a native of Ireland, worked for numerous livestock men in Morrow County around the turn of the century. Little is known of his background.

Campbell: Michael, Patrick, William and Peter Campbell were born in County Longford and arrived in the district around the turn of the century. They engaged in the livestock business and their principal operations were in Gilliam County.

O'Canavan: Peter Canavan was one of the many early Irish who assisted in livestock operations and was probably from County Mayo.

O'Canning: Patrick Canning, one of the later arrivals, worked for many of the livestock men in the neighborhood.

Cantwell: Father Thomas Cantwell, born in County Kilkenny, succeeded Father O'Rourke as parish priest in Heppner in December 1918, died in 1927, and was buried in Ireland.

Carney: Michael J. Carney, born in New Orleans of Irish parents in 1854, arrived in the area in 1882, and for a number of years operated a stage line between Pendleton and Ukiah. Later chief of police in Pendleton and also a deputy sheriff of Umatilla County from 1894 to 1898. Two brothers, Samuel J. and Edward F., were ranchers in the Pilot Rock-Morrow County area.

MacCarthy, MacCarty: James Carty, one of the giants of the Gaels,

Mr. and Mrs. Jeremiah Brosnan, about 1900 (Author's collection).

was an early partner of John Kilkenny and John Sheridan. He was born in County Leitrim in 1854 and emigrated to the Morrow County region in 1890. He owned and operated a substantial sheep and cattle ranch in the Tub Springs area most of his life, losing a substantial portion of his holdings in the Great Depression. His son, Patrick Carty, salvaged the remnants, and at the time of his death in 1955, was a comparatively wealthy man, leaving an estate far in excess of $100,000. Jim married Maria Curran in Ireland in 1898, and from this union was born Pat, previously mentioned, and Ann Smith and Mary Doherty, both now living. Maria died in 1922. At the commencement of World War II, the U. S. Army took over the Carty ranch, including Jim's home. On the occasion of serving the initial papers and on each succeeding occasion, although then in his seventies, he refused to move from his home and chased the members of the Air Corps from the ranch. Being in a quandry, the military sought the assistance of Federal Judge James Alger Fee, by scheduling a formal proceeding before him. At the commencement of the proceeding, the representative of the military outlined, in considerable detail, the difficulties they were having and asked the court for an order of possession with a writ of assistance. After pondering the problem for a few moments, Judge Fee stated: "If the military of the United States cannot dispossess Jim Carty, I won't even try." Fortunately, patriotism and the persuasion of family and friends overcame his will to resist, and saved the military from complete defeat. After forty years he gave up his home, so full of memories of the singing, dancing and fighting Irish, and moved to a new location on Willow Creek.

Con Carty and Willie Carty were brothers of Jim and were in the Morrow area and the livestock business for a considerable period of time.

O'Casey: Charles Casey was one of the many sons of St. Patrick that served in the King's Navy. A rough and ready character that fit in well with the life on the Irish ranches.

Casserly: James Casserly, one of the many from County Leitrim, was a serious dedicated fellow, with a scholarly strain.

O'Cassidy: Michael Cassidy, a strange but intelligent person, was born in County Cavan and devoted his services to the livestock of the Irish in the district for over a quarter of a century.

Clancy: John, William and Mike Clancy arrived in Morrow County in the early part of the century and were born in County Leitrim.

O'Clery: Mildred Clery was a nurse who worked for Dr. A. D. McMurdo in Heppner for a great many years.

Cluff: Edward Cluff was born in Ireland in November, 1829. He arrived in Morrow County about 1870 and took a homestead on which land part of the town of Ione is now located.

Connelen: Bernard, Frank and Patrick Connelan, County Leitrim men, are three members of this sept that reached the Morrow County

territory in the early part of the century and devoted themselves to the livestock industry.

O'Connell: (This sept has produced a great many distinguished persons, including Justice Kenneth J. O'Connell of the Oregon Supreme Court.)

John and Patrick Connell and their sister, Bridget, were born in County Leitrim and arrived in the area within a few years after 1900. John was killed in an unfortunate affair, while Pat engaged in the sheep and other business in the Heppner area for a great many years. Bridget married Pat O'Rourke.

O'Cooney: John C. Cooney arrived in the Condon area in 1882. In 1880 he married Mary Ellen Summers in Winfield, Kansas. He was born in County Tipperary. Nellie Cooney Kennedy and Sylvester Cooney now reside in Condon, while Leon resides in Salem. They are the only surviving children.

O'Connolly: Pat Connolly was a County Leitrim man and although his main operation was in the Wasco County area, he was well known as a sheepman in Morrow County. Anthony J. Connolly is of the same family.

O'Corrigan: Pat Corrigan, a Leitrim man, arrived early in the century and lost a leg in the First World War. He worked principally for the Monahans.

O'Crean, Cregan: Hugh, Michael and Patrick Creegan worked for Michael Kenny after their arrival about 1911, probably from County Donegal.

MacCunneen: Ed Cunnion, from Leitrim, was with the main stream of Irish that arrived either before or immediately after the turn of the century. Like most of the others, he devoted himself to the livestock industry.

Cunningham. Charles Cunningham, one of the magnificent men of the early livestock industry in Morrow and Umatilla counties, was born in County Galway, Ireland, in 1846, landed in New York in 1864, and after serving in the Navy for a considerable period, landed in San Francisco. He took a pre-emption claim on Butter Creek in 1876 and thereafter devoted most of the remainder of his life to the raising of livestock, being at one time president of the Woolgrowers Stock Journal. His first wife was Sarah Doherty, who was a native of Donegal and who died in 1885 leaving a daughter, Sarah. Later, in 1893, he married Katherine Flanagan in Pendleton and to them were born two children, Cecelia, now Cecelia Shannon, and Charles. His name is perpetuated in the Cunningham Sheep Company and Cunningham Sheep & Land Company, the corporations that now own and control all, or practically all, of the old Cunningham holdings.

O'Curran: Rose Ann, Maria and Bridget Curran, of whom the first two arrived in Morrow County in 1898, Rose Ann marrying John Kilkenny and Maria James Carty. Bridget (Bea) arrived in 1908

[27]

and married James Sheridan. John, Joseph, Patrick and Peter were of the same family, mainly arriving in the Morrow County area in the nineties. All were closely connected with the livestock industry. Patrick died at an early age when thrown from a wool wagon.

Michael Curran, employed for close to half a century by the Hughes family, Percy and Edwin, the son and grandson of the great benefactor, William Hughes.

Another Pat Curran, from Leitrim, married Frances Doherty.

Currin: George J. Currin, one of the pioneer livestock operators in the Hinton Creek area. Currinsville, Oregon, was named for George and Hugh Currin, the father and uncle respectively of George J. His sons were Hugh C. and Edward R. His ancestors came from Ireland. Grandsons Hugh, Ralph, George and Bob survive, Ralph being a prominent attorney in Pendleton.

O'Daly: Arthur Daly was a settler on Butter Creek between 1880 and 1890.

James and Michael Daly were born in County Longford. Jim arrived in Morrow County in 1910 and Mike at a later date. Each worked for Mike Kenny and John Kilkenny. Jim married Kathryn McDevitt, who was born in County Donegal. He homesteaded in Newman Canyon and later expanded his holdings, so at the time of his retirement he was a substantial landowner in the Morrow County area. Inquiring, dedicated and intellectual, a sergeant with the gift of a real leader.

Darcy: John Darcy could hold his own with the best of the shepherds and remained in the profession for practically all of his life.

Dennen: James Dennan was another of the clan who originated in County Leitrim and found his way to the County of Morrow.

Dennis: Henry Dennis was a County Leitrim boy, a herder of sheep and an all around ranch hand for many of the Irish employers in Morrow County. His wife Margaret's maiden name was Cook and she was likewise born in Ireland.

O'Devlin: Barney and Mike Devlin from County Donegal enriched the conversation of the times with their plentiful humor and dedication to the cause. Barney was a successful sheepman.

Dillon: Harry Dillon, a man of whom little is known, except that he was thoroughly Irish and was fully accepted in the community.

O'Dolan: James and Pat Dolan arrived about 1907 from County Leitrim. Fannie Dolan arrived somewhat later and married Peter Slevin.

O'Donnelly: James Donnelly, also referred to as Mike, hailed from County Leitrim and spent a substantial part of his life in providing mutton chops for the American market.

O'Donoghue, Donohue: Andy and Mike Donohue on arrival worked on the Kilkenny ranches. Andy successfully engaged in the sheep business for a great many years, but then had his setbacks. Mike married and lived in Pendleton. His wife and children still reside in that community. Mike arrived in the territory around 1910, while Andy was here in 1906. Both were County Leitrim boys.

Dougherty, Doherty: Difficulty is encountered in separating the different Doherty families in the Morrow County area. Without minimizing the importance of each Doherty, I shall select a few individuals for comment and treat the remainder as a group.

B. P. Doherty, a native of Donegal, was a pioneer rancher in Sand Hollow. He arrived in Morrow County with James G. Doherty in either 1885 or 1886. He married Catherine Doherty and to this union were born Bernard P., William, John, Rosella, wife of Alex Lindsay, Catherine, wife of Charles Monagle, Frances, wife of Pat Curran, Dorothy and Lawrence. A wealthy man at the time of his death, his estate has been well cared for and enlarged by his industrious sons and daughters.

Bernard P. (Barney) Doherty, a world traveler, distinguished as a critic of football techniques. He has also demonstrated his deep educational interest by serving on the board of trustees of both the University of Portland and Gonzaga University.

Patrick Doherty, long time patriarch of Big Butter Creek and connoisseur of fine whisky. Properly referred to as the Dean of the Irish when he passed away in 1948. Pat was born in County Donegal and placed his feet in the Morrow County area some time around 1888. At 20 years of age, he started to herd sheep and in 1901 had earned sufficient to return to the land of his birth and claim his sweetheart, Mary McLaughlin, as his bride. Returning to the Doherty headquarters at Vinson, he acquired a band of sheep, started in the sheep business and eventually owned 27,000 acres of land and approximately 6,500 head of sheep. Noted throughout his life for his generosity, integrity and Irish wit, Pat had little difficulty in being thoroughly accepted by the entire Pendleton, Pilot Rock and Heppner area residents. A man of six feet in height and of incredible strength, Pat survived a gunshot wound in his early life that would have killed an ordinary person. To his first marriage were born Joe, Dan and Con and two daughters, Mary, Mrs. J. S. Reimer, and Susan, the wife of Bernard P. Doherty, previously mentioned.

After the death of his first wife, he married Mary Ann Doherty, and to this marriage were born Jack, Emmett, Vincent and Patricia, Mrs. Fred Mutch. Pat never forgot the mother country and returned there in 1901 to marry his first wife, again in 1908 with his wife and three children, and again in 1926 with his then wife. He had five sons, Dan, Con, Jack, Emmett and Vincent in the service in the Second World War. Also in service was a grandson, Joseph.

James G. Doherty, commonly known as "Black Horse" Jim on account of his long residence and land accumulations in Black Horse Canyon in Morrow County, was born in County Donegal and arrived in New York City in 1883. After a brief residence in that city, he made his way to Butter Creek and for the following four

Members of the Edward Doherty-Annie Doherty wedding party, Palace Hotel, Heppner, 1895. 1st row seated: Ed McDaid, Ed Doherty (groom), Annie Doherty (bride), James and Katie Barney Doherty, Pat Kilkenny, Katie Johnson Cornett, Jimmy Johnson, Phil Doherty, Katie and Little Barney Doherty. Top Row standing: Pat Doherty, Mike Marshall, unknown, Frank Kilkenny, Tom Kilfillen, Father Briody, Mike Kenny, Phil Doherty, Mary Doherty Kenny, John Kilkenny, Jim Carty, Charlie Van Winkle, Lame Barney Doherty, Phil and Dan Hirl, Johnny Kenny (boy standing behind Jimmy and Katie Doherty).

years worked for Charley Cunningham. In 1893, he married Catherine M. Doherty, likewise a native of County Donegal. Many of their children are prominent in all walks of life in Morrow County and other places in Oregon. The original home place in Black Horse Canyon is still owned by the family. He was one of the first of the Irish to devote his full attention to the raising of wheat.

Susan (Susie) Doherty. Susan was born in Carnonah in Ireland. On her arrival in this country, around the turn of the century, she married Dillard French, a cattleman, closely related to the fabulous livestock pioneer, Pete French. Dillard was one of the most successful of all cattlemen in eastern Oregon, and at the time of his death had accumulated a large fortune in cattle and land. His sons, Jack and Herb, were outstanding examples of young ranch operators, each acquiring a marked proficiency in the arts of the cowboy, including calf and steer roping and bronco busting. Joe French, son of Herb, is a respected and distinguished lawyer in Umatilla County, while Pete, son of Jack, is one of the leading cattlemen of the area. A daughter, Agnes, married Cleve Walton. Bud Walton, a son of this union, married Catherine Johnson, a daughter of Jimmie, to whom later reference is made. The Waltons were exceptionally successful cattle operators in the Long Creek area. James, a son, and great-grandson of Susan and Dillard, is another distinguished lawyer in the Pendleton area.

Susan Doherty. One of the truly great Irish pioneers. In 1890, when nine years of age, she arrived in Umatilla County. A sister of Big Pat Doherty, she married Charles McDevitt in 1906. Through their joint efforts they put together one of the fine livestock ranches in the area near Gurdane. Renowned as a horsewoman, she consistently took to the range and helped with the cattle and sheep. She could well serve as a model for those who desire an active life with a gracious smile and a touch of charity for all.

Others from this famous clan arriving in the Morrow County area from County Donegal included Bernard, Neil, Dan, William, Charles, Dennis, Red Pat, John (Dutchey), John C. (Taylor) and another John, who operated a saloon in the early days in Heppner. Certainly, this does not exhaust the names of the Dohertys who participated in the early development of the area, but it gives a good sample.

O'Downey: Dan Downey, a purveyor of the spiritous liquors and ranch hand on the Kilkenny ranches for a great many years. Dan's experiences in supplying the wants of the community during the days of Prohibition would in themselves provide excellent material for a book on "How to Avoid the Law."

Doyle, MacDowell: James and Michael Doyle were born in County Leitrim and arrived in the County of Morrow to turn their attention to a life as shepherds early in the century.

[31]

O'Driscoll: Cornelious Driscoll, a native of Ireland, was in and around Heppner for a good many years.

Father Patrick Driscoll, a priest who served in Heppner on occasion while Father Kelly was on leave, also a native of Ireland.

O'Duffy: John Duffy swore by his Irish ancestors in County Donegal and spent many a long day for many a year in moving the sheep from the plains of north Morrow County to the foothills in the south, then on to the peaks and the valleys of the Blues, only to reverse the trail when the snow started to decorate the emerald green of the pines.

Dundas: Jack Dundass, a nephew of John Kilkenny, arrived at the Morrow County ranch from New York around 1908. A son of John's sister, Bridget, and John Dundass, he was one of the most picturesque of all. A cowboy at heart, the tales of his bronco busting prowess and lack of it, are legendary. A veteran of both the Canadian and U. S. armies in World War I, he thrice rose to a sergeancy, but due to a flair for the spectacular and a complete disregard of detail, he ended his service as a private.

> The Private was gay as he sat in his saddle,
> Old Smoky was tense underneath.
> Then off came the hat, and up went the outlaw,
> To sunfish and look for the heath.
> Still doing his best, he reached for the chest,
> With his spurs that were sharp as a razor.
> The outlaw then spun, as though shot from a gun,
> And there was no need for a hazer.

Howard Dundass, his brother, was a principal truck driver on the ranch shortly after World War I.

O'Dunn: William (Billy) Dunn, a native of Ireland, was a long-time resident of the territory and during the latter part of his life was the principal steward at the Elks Lodge in Pendleton.

Edward Dunn, likewise a native of Ireland, was active in the area during the period under scrutiny.

O'Farrelly, Farley: James, Peter and Patrick Farley were of the same family. They were born in Arva, County Longford. Jim arrived in 1898 and for a time was on the Kilkenny ranch and then worked for James Carty. Later he tended camp for Michael Kenny, again worked for James Carty until 1904 when he and his brother, Pat, started in the sheep business and this continued until 1922. Jim married Sarah Kenny in 1907 and to them were born Mary C., John E., James N., Margaret and Roseanna. Jim died in 1958. He was one of the most lovable of the Irish, intellectually brilliant, an ardent student of current affairs, yet a great favorite with the youngsters. Pete was also engaged in the sheep business. One of his sons, J. J. Farley, is an automobile dealer in Heppner at present.

Michael Farley, also born in Ireland, was in the area at the same time. Patrick Gregory Farley, son of Rose Ann Farley Kilkenny, arrived with his mother in 1898.

[33]

Heppner, Oregon, 1893, from the reservoir (OHS collections).

O'Fee, O'Fay: James Albert Fee, a distinguished citizen of Umatilla and Morrow counties, was born in the Midwest, the offspring of Irish parents who were born in County Armagh. A lawyer of exceptional ability, he was one of the youngest circuit judges ever to serve the Sixth Judicial District, which is composed of Umatilla and Morrow counties. Long recognized as one of the great trial lawyers of the Pacific Northwest, he continued his practice until well in his eighties. Few witnesses could stand up under the devastating effect of his cross-examination.

James Alger Fee, son of James Albert, a distinguished lawyer and jurist, who served as circuit judge in Morrow and Umatilla counties from 1929 to 1931, at which time he was appointed judge of the U. S. District Court for Oregon. He served in that capacity from that date until he was elevated to the U. S. Court of Appeals for the Ninth Circuit in 1954, on which court he served until the time of his death. He was, and is, recognized as one of the great jurists of his time.

Chester Fee was another son of James Albert who distinguished himself, not in the law, but in the literary field. Outstanding is his splendid work on the life of Chief Joseph.

Fitzgerald: (Two of the most influential noble families in Irish history are of this name: the County Kildare branch furnished the Dukes of Leinster, known in history as the Earls of Kildare, and the Munster branch was headed by the Earls of Desmond. Other branches of the family settled in Counties Mayo and Waterford. Rightly or wrongly, one of them was accused of destroying the Cathedral on the Rock of Cashel. On being accused, he said, "I would not have done so had I not been told that the Archbishop was inside.")

Thomas Fitzgerald. Although his permanent residence was in Pendleton, he lent no small part of his industrious life to the Heppner and other areas in Morrow County. At one time one of the leaders of the legal profession in that area, he devoted most of his life to serving as a municipal judge or justice of the peace, and for one short period of time as district attorney in the state of Washington. The son of Thomas and Mary (O'Laughlin) Fitzgerald, he crossed the plains by covered wagon in 1846, passing the winter at Whitman Station, leaving shortly before the massacre in 1847. Justice Fitzgerald was serving as justice of the peace during most of the Prohibition days in the Pendleton area and many tall tales are told in connection with the disappearance of the liquid evidence, both before and after a verdict. Nevertheless, the justice remained in the eyes of the community a man of staunch integrity, upright principles and great moral strength.

Fitzmaurice: Maurice Fitzmaurice, born in Daugh, County Kerry, in 1853, the son of Maurice Fitzmaurice and Mary Fisher Fitzmaurice. The family originated in County Kerry. He was a direct descendant of Baron Lixau. He arrived in the U. S. in 1884 and settled on Rowe

[34]

Main street in Heppner 1898. All buildings shown except the Palace Hotel (where it is reported Owen Wister wrote *The Virginian*) were washed away in the 1903 flood. (OHS collections).

Creek, 15 miles from Fossil. Became editor of the Condon *Times* in 1906, a newspaper widely distributed in Morrow County. He was also a sheepman. In later years, he was involved in real estate, was Condon's city judge, served as mayor of the city and was a member of the Oregon Legislature. He died in November, 1936. The children were Kathleen, Mary, Annabella, Maurice and John, all born in Ireland; William Henry, Hannah, Jane, Charles Edward, Robert Massey, and last, but certainly not least, Elizabeth, more commonly known as Elsie Dickson, that lovable personality, sharp-witted conversationalist and distinguished author formerly associated with the *East Oregonian* in Pendleton.

Fitzpatrick: Michael J. Fitzpatrick arrived from Offaly (then Queens) County, at the Kilkenny ranch shortly after the first of the century. He was a dedicated student even when herding sheep, and a delightful companion of the youth of the time. He had what it took, and after marriage to one of the McDevitt girls, acquired a substantial fortune in wheat lands near Ione. Michael J. was truly a fine gentleman.

Flannigan: Patrick and Frank Flannigan took homesteads in Sand Hollow in 1892. The land later became part of the Kilkenny ranch. The homestead was bisected by the Oregon Trail and was one of the principal watering places. Two wells had been sunk on the land long prior to the homestead. The water supply was always known as Flannigan's Wells and was located approximately one mile north of the area which is known as the Sand Hollows Battle Ground, this being an affair between Cornelius Gilliam's Oregon volunteer troops and the Cayuse Indians on February 24 and 25, 1848.

Flood: James Flood was on the Kilkenny Ranch about 1906. He applied for a homestead and was killed while constructing the cabin. A patent to the same land was later issued to John Kelly. Jim was another favorite with the children. Like most of the others, he was born in County Leitrim.

O'Foloy, Foley: John Foley, another of the Leitrim Irish, that found his way to the Kilkenny and other Irish ranches in Morrow County.

Furlong: Henry Patrick Furlong joined the Irish group in the area in the early part of the century. Little, if anything, is known of his background other than that he was born in Ireland.

Gaffney: Mary Gaffney, from Leitrim, previously mentioned, was the wife of Jeremiah Brosnan.

O'Gallagher: Charles and Joseph Gallagher mingled with the tide that flowed into Morrow County both before and after the turn of the century. Nothing else is known.

Gilfillen, Kilfillen: Thomas Gilfillin was born in Leitrim in 1861 and was employed by Michael Kenny at the time of his arrival in the eighties. Later engaged in the sheep business on a ranch about 12 miles south and east of Heppner.

Gilleese: James Gilleese was born in County Leitrim and arrived around the early 1900s. Bridget, his wife, a sister of Peter Farley, now living in Dublin. Joe, a son, lives in Hermiston.

Grant, O'Greany, McGrane: Fred and Michael Grant were each in the mainstream of County Leitrim Irish that herded the flocks and tended the camps on the many Irish sheep ranches of the era.

Gray: Henry Gray put his shoulder to the Irish wheel of fortune in Morrow County around 1909. Born in County Leitrim, he was recognized as one of the outstanding characters of the sept.

MacGuignan: Patrick Guignan was somewhat later than most, arriving in 1912. He was in the area for a number of years following the general activities herein mentioned.

Hackett: James Hackett, a prominent sheepman for many years, was born in Dublin and arrived in the area in the nineties. At his death, a substantial part of his estate was willed to the Pendleton Foundation, the funds later being used in the construction of Pendleton Junior High School.

[36]

O'Halpin: Michael Halpin from Uth in County Meath was a long time herder of sheep for the Kilkennys, Dohertys, Kennys and others.

Halton: John Halton, a County Cavan man, worked for the Irish sheep and wool growers of the area.

Hanrahan: Patrick Hanrahan suddenly appeared in the area and just as suddenly disappeared. Nothing is known of his background.

O'Harkin: Partick Harkins, long-time taxi owner and driver in the Pendleton-Morrow County area, came from Donegal.

O'Hart: Patrick Hart came to Heppner from Donegal in 1909 and first worked on the Kilkenny ranches.

Hartin: Michael Hartin came from County Cavan and was a long-time sheep owner and operator. Leaving that business, he purchased a luxurious hotel in Echo, known as the Town House.

O'Healy: John, Michael and Patrick Healy arrived in Morrow County from County Leitrim in the year 1904. John married Annie Kenny, daughter of Michael, and was a highly successful livestock man. His ranch on Butter Creek is still operated by members of his family. Michael Healy married a daughter of John Hughes, a pioneer Irishman. Mike was engaged in the livery stable business for a number of years and later devoted his attention to forming a portion of the Kilkenny ranches. Pat was likewise engaged in the sheep business. Father Richard Healy was one of the later Irish, being the pastor in Heppner in the mid-thirties.

O'Heffernan: Elizabeth (Betty) Heffernan arrived in the Pendleton area in the twenties, then married Dr. Richard C. Lawrence and moved to Heppner. They resided in that city until after the doctor's death in the late forties. Betty is now the wife of William P. Kilkenny.

O'Hennessy: Father George Hennessy, born in Ireland, served with Father T. J. Brady in Heppner during the visit of the Chapel Car, St. Anthony, on which occasion he was a resident for a considerable period of time.

O'Heslin: Thomas and Michael Heslin worked for a number of the Irish sheep operators in the area.

Hetherton: Frank Heatherton from County Longford, an Irishman of considerable dignity, came to the colony in 1912. A herder of sheep for most of his life in this area.

O'Higgins: James Higgins, known as Gentleman, a bardic soul of limitless imagination.

Another Jim Higgins (Whillet) married Katherine Maguire in the early days of the settlement. An outstanding rancher in MacDonald Canyon. The children, Mary, Kathleen and Jim, attended school in Pendleton.

Phil and Patrick Higgins, two outstanding ranch hands who arrived between 1900 and 1903. All were natives of County Leitrim.

Hirl: Dan and Ned Hirl, both natives of Donegal, arrived in the nineties.

O'Houghton: Mike and Barney Houghton, brothers, arrived in Morrow County from Donegal in the early 1900s and were continuously employed in the Irish settlement.

Hughes, O'Hea, Hayes: William Hughes was born in County Tipperary, Ireland, in 1849. Arriving in America, he spent a number of years in California and journeyed to the Heppner country in the 1870s. After a successful venture in land and livestock, he went to Ireland and returned by water to San Francisco, from there to Portland and then to The Dalles by stage, then on to Heppner. There he engaged in financing farmers and livestock men, including many of the Irish, until 1900 when he moved to Portland. He remained one of the principal financiers of the Morrow County Irish until his death in 1917. Without question, he was one of the prodigious men of his time. His grandson, W. E. Hughes, remains as one of the most successful livestock men in Morrow County; a daughter, Mrs. Lawrence Lutcher, is now residing in Milton-Freewater.

John Hughes, a large, powerful man, a cousin of Bill's, was very successful and owned one of the first automobiles in the area. One of his daughters married Mike Healy.

Matt Hughes, a brother of John, was a successful operator in Heppner.

Hurley: Timothy Hurley, probably from County Cork, roamed the foothills south of Heppner for many years prior to his death and burial in the cemetery of that city in 1898.

Johnson, MacKeon: Felix Johnson, a native of County Leitrim, arrived in Morrow County at the same time as Jeremiah Brosnan. Felix, and later his two sons, James and Felix, operated a large cattle ranch between the middle and north forks of the John Day River. Their families are still operating these properties.

John H. Johnson was born on the high seas in 1846 to his parents, Hiram and Nancy E. Johnson, who were born in County Clare. He crossed the plains in 1871. After the death of his first wife in 1894, he married Nancy E. Hardman, the widow of David N. Hardman, after whom the town of Hardman in Morrow County was named, the community being previously known as Midway.

Kane: Patrick Kane took a homestead where the cemetery is now located on Little Butter Creek, approximately five miles downstream from Lena. Little more is known of his background.

Kavanagh, Kavanaugh: Dr. Henry J. Kavanaugh, while practicing in Pendleton, had an extensive acquaintanceship and practice throughout the Morrow County area. A fine gentleman and an excellent physician, Dr. Kavanaugh is survived by a son and daughter living in Phoenix, Arizona, as well as daughters living in Baker, Oregon and Keokuk, Iowa.

Keating: Michael Keating, Civil War veteran and long-time resident of Pendleton, had many contacts and was widely known by the Irish of Morrow County. The same can be said of his son, Tom,

a dedicated member of the American Legion with, at times, a gargantuan thirst for the spiritous liquors.

Keegan, MacEgan: John and Frank Keegan, County Leitrim boys, were in the full flow of Irish tide to Morrow County at, or near, 1900. Before becoming sheepmen in their own right they worked on the Kenny, Kilkenny, Carty and other ranches. A member of this family was one of the plaintiffs in a famed sheep conversion case before the Oregon Supreme Court and reported in *171 Or. 194.*

Kelleher: Michael Kelleher joined the Morrow County group in 1898. He completely disappeared from the scene a number of years later.

O'Kelly: Father Michael J. Kelly was the first Irish priest in St. Patrick's Parish at Heppner. He arrived in 1898, at which time his parish extended to Mayville, Spray, Fossil and Condon. Born in Ireland, he was a great organizer and a true evangelist.

John J. Kelly was born in County Leitrim and made his way to the Morrow County Irish in 1909. Worked on the Kilkenny ranches and later acquired his own livestock. For the last twenty years of his life, he was an outstanding sheep and wool buyer, finding his way to his God in an unfortunate stairway accident in the Packard Hotel in Pendleton in January, 1940.

O'Kennedy: William and Margaret Quinn Kennedy were born in County Wexford and arrived in the Hermiston area to take desert land entries about 1910. Jack Kennedy, son of William and Margaret, was a noted wrestler in the Heppner area, at one time champion of the middleweight division, and wrestled Jim Londus, one time world champion, in Heppner some fifty years ago. Jack married Nellie Cooney.

Warren Kennedy was around Heppner for a great many years, working at many odd jobs.

O'Kenny: Michael Kenny was born in County Leitrim and arrived in Morrow County in 1883. He married Mary Doherty, a sister of James, in 1884. To this union were born John F., Sarah, Rose Ann, James T., Joseph B. and Cecelia. Mike was an exceptionally successful businessman and left a very substantial estate. Furthermore, he was one of the toughest of Irishmen, having survived the shock of a bolt of lightning that killed the team of horses which he was driving. John Kenny, a brother of Michael, arrived in Umatilla County in the early eighties. He first worked at a stagecoach stop located at the foot of what is commonly known as Franklin Hill and later drove stagecoach between Heppner and Pendleton. He took a homestead in what is commonly known as Mud Springs Canyon and sold this homestead to Hugh Fields. He returned to Ireland and took care of the family farm and his grandfather in the early part of the century. James Kenny, a long-time foreman at the Cunningham Sheep Company and Kilkenny ranches. One of the intellectuals of the group, with a flair for fine clothing and intelligent conversation, even if it

[41]

Michael Kenny family, with John, Sarah, James, Annie and Joseph in the back row; Mrs. Kenny (Mary), Cecelia, and Michael Kenny in the front (Author's collection).

was with himself. His brother, Barney, was in the Morrow County area for a number of years.

Kiernan, Kernan, MacTiernan: John Kiernan, long-time cattleman and employee of the Voglers and the Kilkennys, was born in County Leitrim. John was a dedicated worker and probably knew cattle as well as any man in eastern Oregon. Arthritis and advancing age joined to place him in a hospital for the aged in Pendleton.

Dennis, James and Martin Kiernan were others of this sept who lent their labors to the sheep and cattle ranchers of the county.

J. M. Kernan was the station agent and telegraph operator for the O.W.R.&N. Co. in Heppner at the time of the Heppner flood in 1903. He, his wife Mary, and their two children were drowned in the flood.

Kilbride, MacBride: Patrick Kilbride arrived in Morrow County from County Leitrim and worked for James Carty and other sheepmen early in the century.

Kilkenny: John Kilkenny has already been discussed.

Frank Kilkenny, a brother of John, was born in County Leitrim in 1871 and died in Morrow County in 1933. He married Margaret Brady in 1900 in Heppner. To this union were born John W., Francis (usually called Frank), Della (Mrs. Joseph Wilson, now deceased), Martha (Mrs. James Doyle), Camilla (Mrs. James Monahan), Joseph (now deceased) and Peggy (Mrs. John Paulson), all born in Ireland. Peter and Molly (Mrs. John Doherty) were born in Morrow County. Both Peter and Molly are deceased, Peter having been electrocuted in a subway accident in New York City. The children that were in the Morrow County area were Frank, Peggy, Joe, Camilla, Molly and Peter. John W. and Camilla are still in the Heppner area. Frank was highly successful in the sheep business before he sold out and returned to Ireland, where he purchased a farm and family residence, Fihorra. He returned to Ireland in 1906 and then to Morrow County in 1928.

Pat Kilkenny was likewise John's brother and the tallest of the three. He also operated a sheep ranch in the Sand Hollow area at the same time as Frank. They either returned to Ireland together, or within a short time of each other. Pat returned to the ancestral home, Bundarrah, where his son, Frank, now lives and in which his father, Peter, his grandfather, John, his great-grandfather and Paul, his great-great-grandfather were born. It would seem that the home Bundarrah, signifying end of the oaks, has been in the family since the time of James Kilkenny who was attainted by William of Orange after the Battle of the Boyne in 1691. Continuing the ancestral occupation are Patrick and Eileen, Frank's son and daughter.

Lane: Hughie and Frank Lane were brothers, natives of Ireland, arriving in Morrow County in the early days of the century. Hughie, an excellent sheepman when away from the booze, was the deadbeat of all deadbeats when on a spree. On such occasions, his gargantuan thirst could be satisfied only by the purse of a Rockefeller. He matched his lack with never to be paid loans from the uninitiated.

O'Leary: John and Patrick Leary were among the hundreds who entered the settlement of the Irish in the Sand Hollow and Willow Creek areas.

O'Lee: John and Patrick Lee. Johnny Lee, for a quarter of a century or longer, operated a pastime in Pendleton. Previously, he was part of the Irish tide that had swept into the county to the west. Pat Lee was in the same area and performed similar functions as his fellow nationals.

O'Lennon: John Lennon, one of the taller and more powerful Irishmen, first put his feet on the soil of Morrow County about 1914. A portrait of dedication and modesty, John has disdained the semi-annual sprees of many and acquired a tidy little fortune.

Frank, Con, James, Pat and Peter Lennon arrived in Morrow County shortly after John.

O'Lonergan: Patrick Lonergan, a civil engineer, was responsible for building a substantial portion of the first paved highway between Heppner and Pendleton. A famed left halfback at the University of Illinois, he was in a constant bicker with his brother, Frank, a captain of an early Notre Dame team, over the merits of the respective institutions. Pat finished out his life as a very successful life insurance agent, while Frank was an eminent circuit judge in Multnomah County at the time of his death.

O'Loughlin: Bob Laughlin, likewise a comparative newcomer, married Ilene Kilkenny. His son, Robert, is presently assisting in the management of one of the ranches.

MacGovern: James and Michael MacGovern were County Leitrim lads who joined the settlement in Morrow County before 1910.

MacInerney, McInerny: Hugh and John MacInerney were early of the century arrivals, who did their part in the building of the livestock empires of the Irish of the county. Hugh, although short in stature, was noted for his strength.

MacManus: John P. MacManus was an outstanding journalist, editor and publisher. He published the *Northwest Livestock and Woolgrowers Journal,* an illustrated monthly, for a number of years and was particularly well known by, and interested in, the livestock operators in Morrow and Umatilla counties.

McCabe, MacCabe: Those of this sept who found their way from County Leitrim to Morrow around 1901, and shortly thereafter, were Frank, Mike, Luke, Pat, Phil, John and their sister, Anne. At one time Frank was the proud possessor of over 10,000 head of sheep. Another McCabe family, unrelated to the above, but from the same county, included Pete, Mike and Jimmy.

McCartin, MacCarton: John and Thomas McCartin left County Leitrim and arrived in 1909 to shepherd the flocks of the Kilkennys and others. Frank McCartin was from the same general area and was

[43]

related to John and Tom. He was one of the principal figures in the capture of the murderers of Til Taylor, famed sheriff of Umatilla County. Barney Devlin, previously mentioned, was with McCartin at the time. The latter arrived about 1908.

McCarty, MacCarty: David McCarty was born in Ireland on March 17, 1832, and entered Oregon in 1863. In 1877 he purchased 200 acres of land on Butter Creek, where his descendants still live. He settled at McMinnville before arriving on Butter Creek. His children were John A., James A., Mary H., William A. and Otis.

Jim McCarty arrived in the area from County Cork. As with most of the others, he assisted the sheep barons in their year-round labors.

Howard McCarty was a roustabout laborer in Heppner who roomed at the Star Hotel for a number of years.

McCarmack, MacCormack: Father Francis McCormack, although a comparative latecomer, served the Irish of Morrow County for a great many years. His dedication to service was mainly responsible for the construction of the new Catholic church in Heppner. He was born in County Longford.

McCullough, MacCullough: Thomas McCullough was born in Ireland on May 20, 1830. He arrived on Willow Creek in Morrow County from San Francisco in 1888. He was the uncle of Jack, Dave, Sam, Bob, Minnie and Sar McCullough.

McDaid, MacDaid: Edward, Jeremiah and Patrick McDaid were early arivals from Donegal. Ed and Jeremiah were successful ranchers in the Juniper Canyon area and a well known spring in that canyon carries the name McDaid. Ed arrived in America in 1898 and his future wife, Ellen Doherty, arrived the same year.

McDermot: Michael McDermot was a County Kerry man and worked as a shepherd for Robert Stanfield when he was not operating a barber shop in the little community of the same name. Pat McDermont was from County Mayo and worked for Barney Doherty and many others.

McDevitt, MacDevitt: Charles McDevitt arrived in Umatilla County from County Donegal in 1904. Met and married Susan Doherty, a sister of Big Pat, in 1906. With his wife, put together one of the fine ranches in the Gurdane area.

Barney, Dan and John McDevitt were the male leaders of this group in Morrow County, arriving around 1905. They were very active in the Ione, Lexington and Juniper Canyon areas in wheat farming and livestock. The family owned the first pneumatic tire equipped motor truck in Morrow County.

McEntire, MacIntyre: John, James and Peter McEntire arrived before the turn of the century, while Thomas, Patrick, Michael, Edward and Miles, unrelated to the former, arrived between 1903 and 1906. All were from County Leitrim. At one time, John was a prominent sheepman owning a ranch on Hinton Creek approximately five miles from Heppner. After helping with the livestock for many, many years, Jim returned to the old country and Pete purchased a ranch near Beaverton. The ranch is now one of the city's beautiful urban areas. Jim married and after his death, Pete returned to Ireland and married the widow. He survives and, at the age of 87, carries the same brilliant mind that trapped the coyote, snared the rabbit, outfoxed the antelope and brought down the goose. This entire McEntire clan came from Leitrim. Another John McIntyre from the same county was in the area at the same time.

McGill: Tom Gill, a Donegalian, an early settler, returned to Ireland in the twenties. His sister, Sarah, married Tom McNamee.

McGinnis, McGenis, MacGinnis: Patrick McGinnis spent most of his life in Grant County, but was well known in Morrow. He was the father of Gertrude McGinnis O'Rouke, who married John O'Rourke. The son, Peter, is now a prominent livestock man in Grant County.

McGrath, MacGrath: Bishop Joseph F. McGrath was born in Kilmacow, County Kilkenny, being the son of James McGrath and Margaret O'Farrell McGrath. Bishop McGrath served the Diocese of Baker County, which included Morrow County, for many years. He administered the Sacrament of Confirmation to many of the Irish youngsters of the county.

McHugh: John McHugh was one of the earliest of the Irish to settle in the Boardman area. A partner with James McNamee in the sheep business, he returned to Ireland after spending the greater part of his life in Morrow County.

McKenna, MacKenna: Father P. J. McKenna, a God-fearing man and a Jesuit who unselfishly served his parishioners in Umatilla and Morrow counties for over a quarter of a century.

Michael and Patrick McKenna, from County Leitrim, planted their stout bodies and stronger hearts in the community in 1907.

McLaughlin, MacLoughlin: Cornelious (Cor) N. McLaughlin, a boy of 16, found his way from Cardonough in County Donegal to the Big Pat Doherty ranch in 1908. With him was Paul Doherty from the same county. Cor married Mary Doherty from Blackhorse Canyon in 1915 and to this union were born 13 children, nine boys and four girls, most of whom remain in the immediate area. Cor was a brother of Big Pat's first wife.

James A. McLaughlin, another stalwart from Donegal, was one of the pioneers who worked for the railroad. His wife, Katie, was a sister of Big Pat. Martin McLaughlin, a brother of James, a longtime resident and leader in the Irish community. Margaret, one of his daughters, a dedicated student of Irish history.

McNally, MacNally: Frank McNally departed from County Longford in 1906 and arrived in the Morrow community in the same year. First he was in the livestock business and for the last 25 years of his life was the owner and operator of a restaurant in Pendleton. Earlier, in 1912, he operated a saloon in Heppner in partnership with John Keegan.

[45]

McNamee, MacNamee: James, John, Mary, Pete, Matt, Dennis and Tom McNamee belong to the County Leitrim group and reached Morrow from 1908 to 1911. Most of the men worked with the livestock. Mary was a delightful and dedicated domestic in the Kilkenny home in Sand Hollow for a number of years. She is married and lives in Portland.

McMenamin, MacMenamin: Frank J. McMenamin was born in Dekalb, Illinois, the son of Patrick McMenamin, a native of County Tyrone. Frank practiced his chosen profession of law in Heppner for a good many years, had many Irish clients and was one of the leaders of the community for a substantial period of time. His son, Robert W. McMenamin, is now a practicing lawyer in Portland.

McVay, MacVeagh: Pat McVay was one of the earlier arrivals in the Irish colony. Many of the Irish sheep lords had the benefit of his services.

MacAvinny, McAvennia: Bridget, Mary and Bernard McVennia were comparative latecomers to Morrow County. Bridget married John Lee, the owner and operator of a prominent pastime in Pendleton. Mary married Dan McDevitt, son of the pioneer Barney McDevitt of Juniper Canyon. Bernard worked in the livestock business and died, unmarried, in 1934.

Madden, O'Madden, Madigan: John Madden arrived in the Lonerock area and was the first settler at that place. His ancestors came from Ireland. A son, George, was the first white child born in Gilliam County. A daughter, Mrs. Robert Blue, lived until recently on the original homestead. Her twin brother, John Madden, lives in Hermiston. The wife of the original John was the first postmistress of Lonerock.

Maguire, MacGuire: Michael and Catherine Maguire, brother and sister, were welcomed into the Morrow community from Leitrim shortly after 1900. Mike, now in his late eighties, was a strip of a man who could hold his own with the giants. Catherine married James Higgins.

Robert F. Maguire, a famed Portland lawyer who rode the eastern Oregon circuit, and wined and dined with and defended famed outlaws and cattle thieves of the Morrow and Grant area, is still living and practicing in the City of Roses. An intellectual progeny of Fermanagh ancestry, he is considered one of the great trial lawyers of the era.

Mahaffy, MacAfee: Little is known of Charles Mahaffy, a migrant laborer who was listed in the Heppner directory of 1912.

Mahoney, O'Mahoney, Mahony: Thomas J. and William P. Mahoney were brothers who engaged in the banking business in Heppner. Thomas J. brought his talents to the First National Bank of Heppner at an early date. When he moved to Portland his brother took charge of the banking affairs in that city. They were sons of Michael Mahoney who was born in County Cork, while their mother,

Catherine Lyons, was born in the same county. Still living in the neighborhood is Phil Mahoney, son of William P., a delightful companion, a dedicated hunter and an excellent trial lawyer. Kathleen Mahoney Mather, a sister of Phil's, is teaching school in Pendleton.

Marshall: Michael and John Marshall were natives of County Louth. They settled in the Castle Rock area on the south side of the Columbia River and were engaged in the livestock business from the mid-nineties well into the first quarter of the present century.

Martin, Gilmartin: Edward Martin, one of the better educated of the early group, left County Cavan and arrived in the district south of the Columbia in 1909. A "dandy" among the Irish, he was envied for his exploits with the fair sex and damned when the venture proved a success. The long winter nights provided plenty of time to speak of his conquests, while the short winter days were tailored to his violent dislike of manual labor.

Milarkey: Thomas Milarkey and Elizabeth Ryan Milarkey were long-time residents of the district. Thomas was born in County Donegal and Mrs. Milarkey was born in Westmeath. They arrived in the area when all eastern Oregon was one county, he in 1860 and she about 1862. Born to this union was Elizabeth Milarkey, now Mrs. Joseph P. Murphy, one of the most gracious of women and a person who has dedicated most of her life to the service of humanity.

Mitchell: John and Patrick Mitchell were born in County Leitrim and were among the early arrivals. Later John married Rose O'Brien.

Mollohan: James, John, Pat, Barney and Matt Mollohan were of the Leitrim group who joined their fellow countrymen around Heppner before 1910. Bee Mollohan, wife of John F. Kenny, arrived at a somewhat later date. Pat served with gallantry as the town marshal of Heppner for over a decade.

Monagle, MacMonagle: Charles Monagle departed from County Donegal in 1910 and arrived in Morrow County the same year. He married Catherine Doherty and was immediately a successful rancher.

Monahan: John, Frank and Pete Monahan provided more than their share of the aggressiveness which at one time made the Irish so prominent in the Morrow-Gilliam County neighborhood. They were sons of Michael and Katherine Kilkenny Monahan. Frank arrived in the United States in 1895, spent his first five years in Boston and Omaha, thence to Morrow County in 1900. In 1903, he moved into the livestock business with James Murtha and in 1913 moved to the Heppner-Willow Creek area. In 1917 he married Marie Farley, a native of County Longford. John, armed as he was with a charming personality, was a long-time power in Gilliam County politics, but has resided in Heppner for many years past.

Moore: Walter E. Moore, still living, a lovable character and distinguished assistant cashier of the First National Bank of Heppner and later manager of the Pendleton Production Credit Association, was

[47]

George Currin and family, in front of their Heppner home, about 1905 (Author's collection).

connected with the livestock industry of the district in question for close to half a century. His grandfather was born in County Tyrone, Ireland, while his grandmother was born in County Armagh. They emigrated to Quebec, Canada, in 1820. Walter's father and mother, Mary Fallon, were born in Huntington County, Quebec. Walter is now serving as U. S. Jury Commissioner for eastern Oregon.

Moran: Eugene (Damo) Moran, one of the many from County Leitrim. Here was a typical example of an Irish giant with huge hands and gigantic feet.

Mulally: Patrick Mullally joined the community early in the settlement, but nothing is known of his background. He passed from the scene many years ago.

Mulligan, O'Mulligan: Owen, Ed and Pat Mulligan put their hands to

[48]

the pitchfork for the Irish overlords in Morrow County between 1905 and 1907. All were from County Leitrim. Harry and Mike Mulligan were from County Cavan.

Jack Mulligan, the jovial music house operator of Pendleton, made Heppner his headquarters for many sojourns in that county. Well acquainted with all the Irish, Jack with his engaging personality and off the cuff jokes, had little trouble strumming up trade with his fellow Celts. His widow, Ruth Ann, and his son, John, continue to operate the music house.

Murphy: To name a few of the Murphys who contributed their mental and physical talents to the Kilkenny and other ranches, I mention Con, Pat, Ben and John. They were natives of County Leitrim.

Edward and Joseph Murphy, long prominent in Pendleton business and politics, had many contacts with the Morrow County Irish. Their father was born in County Wicklow and their mother in Kildare. Ed arrived in the general area around 1890, while Joe arrived in 1902. Mrs. Joe Murphy, the former Elizabeth Milarkey, survives.

W. H. and Daniel Murphy were brothers who took companion homesteads on the plateau between Butter Creek and Sand Hollow. Little is known of their background except they were of Irish ancestry and, for their day, were expert metal workers.

Murtha, Murtagh: James Murtha was born in County Longford and first worked in the New England states before locating in Heppner in May, 1900. After working for James Carty and Pat McDaid, he started on his own. He was financed by another Irishman, Thomas Quaid, to whom later reference will be made. Returning to Ireland in 1919, he married Kathleen Cantwell, a sister of Father Thomas Cantwell, the Heppner parish priest previously mentioned. Highly successful in the livestock business, Jim has been resting on his laurels for a number of years, leaving his children in charge of the substantial ranch properties.

Neville: James Neville of Limerick was a long-time Heppner resident. Knowledge of his background is scanty.

O'Brien: Thomas, Patrick, Rose and Katherine O'Brien, from Leitrim, of course, were all in Morrow before 1910. Rose married John Mitchell, while Katherine married Pat Campbell. Tom, sheepman and successful rancher whose children have followed his pattern, married Lucy Corrigal, the daughter of that very prominent Scot, M. S. Corrigal.

J. P. O'Brien was general passenger agent for the O. W. R. & N. Company, a long-time friend and benefactor of the Heppner Irish and the Oregon vice-president for the American-Irish Historical Society of New York for over a quarter of a century.

O'Connor: Jeremiah, Timothy, Michael, James and Brian O'Connor, all were accustomed to the beauties of County Kerry before pointing their flight of destiny toward the area both north and south of Heppner. Highly successful as livestock operators, Jeremiah and

Jim cashed in on their holdings and returned to the ring of their ancestral county after being in Oregon close to half a century. Brigit was another of the sept who enjoyed the levity and shared the sorrows of an era which is gone forever.

O'Donnell: Thomas O'Donnell, a County Leitrim man, roamed the ranges with the sheep, the cattle and the horses of the Kilkennys, Cartys and Kennys.

Harry T. O'Donnell, a comparative latecomer, was engaged in the restaurant business in Heppner. His long residence in that city and his generosity with the oft times poverty stricken herders made him a figure of respect and admiration. His wife, Claire, will long be remembered for her gracious smiles and helping hands. H. T., Jr. and Russell, sons of Harry, resided in Heppner with their parents— Russell now being deceased.

O'Meara: J. P. O'Meara, a resident of Heppner, and a blacksmith by trade.

O'Neill: Pete and Barney O'Neill found their way to Oregon from County Leitrim around 1904. Pete was a giant in a pigmy's clothing. Although never weighing above 120 pounds, he handled the axes, sledgehammers, and pitchforks with the same efficiency as his towering companions. The author, at age 13 on the occasion of his mother's funeral, wore Pete's blue serge suit.

O'Reiley, O'Reilly: Pat Reiley (Shan to most of his friends), a native of Leitrim, spent most of his life on the hills and vales of Big Butter Creek while in the employ of Big Pat Doherty. Michael O'Reiley, from the same vicinity, spent most of his life in and around Heppner.

Frank, James, Philip, Mike and Francis all came from the same area and arrived before 1910.

Bishop Charles Joseph O'Reilly, Bishop of Baker from June 1903 until March 1919, was a frequent visitor to the Heppner area and, during that period, confirmed most of the first generation Irish of the time. Bishop O'Reilly was a distinguished clergyman and was notable for his keen interest in the establishment and management of parochial schools. Although Bishop O'Reilly was born in St. Johns, New Brunswick, Canada, his ancestors were born in Ireland. His first visit to Heppner was in 1904.

O'Rourke: John O'Rourke was foreman on the Kilkenny ranches for over a decade. He could throw a diamond hitch on a pack animal with the finesse of a master. Sharp of mind and tongue, he had no hesitancy in slashing to ribbons the slow and the dumbwitted. He married Gertrude McGinnis, and as previously mentioned, is survived by his son, Peter.

Hughey O'Rourke was at one time one of the successful sheepmen of the area. He is still living. At times he was more than a bit of a knave, but he had the heart of a saint. At the same time, he had a gargantuan taste for booze and a sharp eye for the women.

[50]

William O'Rourke, a nephew of Father P. J. O'Rourke, was an educated man who married Ida Walters of Pendleton and has many survivors throughout the states. In Heppner, he served as a clerk in Minor & Co., a dry goods store, and later gave his services to the ranchers before moving to Pendleton and establishing an important position with Smythe & Lonergan. He was the father of Robert E. O'Rourke, now a notable practicing lawyer in Pendleton.

Charles, a brother of John, after spending the early part of his American years on the Morrow ranches, then acted as a teamster on the construction of the McKay Dam in the early twenties.

Pete was a brother of Hughey. Barney worked with the others on the ranches of the era. All were born in County Leitrim.

Father Patrick J. O'Rourke succeeded Father Kelly in the Heppner parish in 1912. He served the parish for many years.

O'Shannon: Lee Shannon, an outstanding civil engineer, graduate of the University of Notre Dame in 1912, was very active in the professional field in Morrow and Umatilla counties in the twenties. A man of great personal charm and ability, he was principally responsible for the technical engineering on the many road and highway systems developed in the area, in particular many of the details of the Heppner-Lena-Pendleton highway. Although he and his parents were born in Ontario, Canada, his grandparents were born in Counties Antrim and Tyrone in Ireland. His immediate ancestors included a minister from Canada to France and a general in the Mexican army. Lee married Cecelia Cunningham, previously mentioned.

Quaid, McQuaid, MacQuaid: Thomas, Michael and Patrick Quaid were in the Heppner area long before the turn of the century. They were eminently successful in livestock and wheat farming. Pat Quaid was a member of the original committee that selected the site for the first Catholic church in Heppner in 1887.

Quinlan, O'Quinlan: John Quinlan was a member of the original committee formed to select the site for the first Catholic church in Heppner. His name first appears in Morrow County around 1887. Nothing is known of his background.

Quinn, O'Quinn: Another duo furnished to the ranchers around Heppner by County Leitrim was Patrick and Frank Quinn. As with most of the others, their sojourn was lengthy and their efforts rewarding.

Russell: William J. Russell was born in Belfast, Ireland, in 1843. After immigrating to Missouri with his family, he fought in the Civil War and there lost two brothers. Bill attained considerable prominence as a railroad contractor, his last contract being on the Oregon Short Line through Boise, Idaho. There on October 20, 1883, he married Kate Summers. The following year they moved to Gilliam County where he settled on Matley Flats. For a great many years he drove a six-mule team, hauling wool to, and heavy freight from,

John Sheridan, 1900 (Author's collection).

Arlington, then known as Alkali Flats. Later he acquired a sub-stantial sheep and cattle ranch, which is still in the family. Mrs. Frank Maddock, Mrs. John Monahan, Mrs. John Kilkenny and Ed Russell were born to this union.

Ryan: Elizabeth Ryan (see Milarkey).

Sheridan, O'Sheridan: John and James Sheridan were brothers, John arriving before 1900. As a partner with John Kilkenny and James Carty, he was highly successful and after taking Margaret Brady as a bride, returned to Ireland where he remained for a good many years. He returned to America and died of influenza during the epidemic of 1919. His son, Ed, has for many years been a resident of Pendleton. James Sheridan, also a successful rancher, moved to the Milton-Freewater area after spending many years of his life in Morrow County. He married Brigit Curran. Their married daughters Ann and Molly live near the Washington state line. Other Sheridans placing their stout feet on the soil of Morrow were Hughie and Tom, together with Black Jim. Hughie arrived much later than the others. All were County Leitrim men.

Shields, Shiel, O'Shiel: Michael Shields, a man of the world and of fixed ideas, used his well modulated Irish brogue on the cooks of his day and in the banter of the evening.

Skelly: Luke Skelly came from the then Queens County, was killed by Indians in 1879.

Slevin, O'Slevin: Peter Slevin, the tallest of all the Morrow County Celts, was a highly successful baron. He married Fannie Dolan of County Longford. After many years of dedicated public service in the Boardman area, he sold his flocks and returned to the isle of his birth.

[52]

Smith: John and Frank Smith were part of the Celtic tide that spilled over the area around 1900. Although working on ranches for many years, they were known principally as saloon keepers.

Spillane: Dennis and Patrick Spillane never mentioned the county of their birth, but proud they were of being Irish. The tending of livestock was their principal occupation.

Stack: Father P. J. Stack served the Heppner Celts for a substantial period. His birthplace in Ireland was County Kerry.

Sullivan: Patrick Sullivan was another who served his time on the hills and in the valleys of the county, but little is known of his background.

Summers: Michael Summers, born in County Kilkenny, arrived in New Orleans in 1856 and a few years later married Mary Ellen MacCormack of Tipperary. Michael died in 1860 and in 1863, Mrs. Summers made her way to Oregon with three of her children, where shortly thereafter they took homesteads near Matley Flats. The offspring of this prolific pair now number in excess of 400 persons, including many who are distinguished in the fields of education, politics, religion, engineering and others. Among the outstanding offspring were Kate Summers Russell and Mary Ellen Summers. Children of Kate included Edward Russell, Sudie Maddock, Mrs. John (Margaret) Monahan and Lottie Kilkenny. The original Mrs. Michael Summers was a truly remarkable person.

Walsh: Father John Walsh served in the Heppner parish in the year 1903, while Father Kelly was on leave.

Ward, MacWard: Bernard and William Ward were Leitrim men, while Pat and Jim were from Longford. Barney was one of the most intellectual and dedicated of the entire Irish group. A long-time soothsayer and orator, Barney belongs on the pedestal of achievement of the Irish of Morrow County. Many an adult tear was shed when he was placed to rest on the hill above Heppner in September, 1961. He was truly the friend of all.

Whitney: James, Michael and William Whitney, all from County Longford, lent their tall frames and lean bodies to the cause from the forepart of the century for 25 years or longer. Stouthearted men, they asked and gave no quarter.

Williams: James, Patrick, Peter and John Williams took an early swing around the livestock ranches of the Irish and later proceeded to the Ontario country where they met with further success.

Wilson: Willie Wilson and his wife arrived in Heppner before 1910 with their children James, Dave, Bob, Isabel, Alex and Hannah. Also along was Big Bob. Practically from the beginning, Willie operated a lodging house which catered almost 100 per cent to the Irish of the area. The scene of tremendous brawls during the spring and fall layoffs, the hotel was also a gathering place for the timid, the forlorn and the unemployed. Truly, it was for the Irish a haven in time of need.

State Meeting, Ancient Order of Hibernians
Heppner, Oregon, February, 1914

1. E. H. Deery; 2. John Brosnan; 3. John Kenny; 4. Rev. P. J. O'Rourke; 5. J. H. Peare; 6. Bishop C. J. O'Reilly; 7. —; 8. —; 9. —; 10. — Peare; 11. John F. Kenny; 12. Dennis McNamee; 13. Phil Higgins; 14. Black J. Sheridan; 15. —; 16. —; 17. James Doherty; 18. Ed Doherty; 19 —; 20. Jim Farley; 21. Jerry Brosnan; 22. Mike Marshall; 23. Pat Curran; 24. Frank Monahan; 25. Tom Gill; 26. Paddy Mollahan; 27. Owen Mulligan; 28. Jim McNamee; 29. John Doherty; 30. Michael Kenny; 31. John J. Dundass; 32. Frank Smith; 33. Jim Gillese; 34. Hugh O'Rourke; 35. W. E. O'Rourke; 36. Barney Doherty; 37. Frank McCabe; 38. Jim Williams; 39. John Byrne; 40. Tom Sheridan; 41. Phil Hirl; 42. Spot Curran; 43. James Sheridan; 44. Jim Higgins; 45. John S. Kilkenny; 46. John Brady; 47. Paddy Mulligan; 48. Pat Ward; 49. —; 50. —; 51. Pete Farley; 52. Willy Cunningham; 53. James Higgins; 54. Willy Carty; 55. —; 56. Tim O'Connor; 57. Dutchey Doherty; 58. Con McLaughlin; 59. B. P. Doherty; 60. B. P. Doherty, Jr.; 61. John F. Kilkenny (on the occasion of his first public recitation); 62. Ed Veach; 63. Mickey Currin; 64. John Healy; 65. Mike Doherty; 66. Pete O'Rourke; 67. Pat McDermott; 68. Con Carty; 69. Pat Farley; 70. Barney Ward; 71. Mike Healy; 72. —; 73. John Currin; 74. — O'Connor; 75. John Monahan; 76. Jim Whitney; 77 —; 78. Willy Whitney; 79. John Doherty; 80. Pat McVeah; 81. —; 82. John Keegan; 83. —; 84. John McHugh; 85. Dan McDevitt; 86. —; 87. Tom O'Brien; 88. John O'Rourke; 89. —; 90. John Connell; 91. John McNamee; 92. —.

(Morrow County Courthouse in background.)

Kilkenny Sand Hollow ranch house, about 1910 (Author's collection).

INDEX